GW00373941

KITTICULTURE

written and illustrated by

DAVID WESTWOOD

TWO HEADS PUBLISHING

WELCOME
TO THE
WONDERFUL
WORLD OF
CATS...

SMUDGE

Thanks to
John Berley, Robert Bloomfield, Janet Bonthron,
Sharon Dirnberger, Marilyn Fleming, Charles Frewin, Rudy Garza,
Susan Kelly, Kathy Toguchi and the resources of the vast
Toguchi Cat Library, Mike Rossi, and of course little Schmickels.

Predator!

Self-reliant like the cat — that takes its prey to privacy,
the mouse's limp tail hanging like a shoelace from its mouth.
— *Marianne Moore*

*U*nlike the other slave animals, whose instincts, such as they are, have become decadent, corrupt or just atrophied into uselessness, cats remain what we always were: a pursuer, a raptor. Certainly we can manage without live food — some of us even prefer to — but in a split second we can still switch from Tabby to Tiger, Manx to Lynx. And this is not mere regression. We, the proud, direct descendants of *Felis silvestris libyca* never lost those instincts, and they lie latent behind our every liquid move, ready for resurrection.

As we pour ourselves through the garden fence we're padding across grasslands of which we are the landlord and everything else just tenants on sufferance. As we doze in front of the fire we're reliving our best catches. Our actions with the ball of wool are honing our attack reflexes, and only *seem* like playfulness. And every meal we eat reminds us of our primal directive. We will only ever be *semi*-civilised, and that's the way we like it.

So it should be no surprise to our host species that we revert occasionally, perhaps even regularly, to hunting mode. It's in our genes, our natures, our souls. Cats are natural selection's best land predator, kin to the air's eagle and the ocean's shark. Not for nothing is the lion known as the King of the Jungle (though it should be *Queen*, since it's the lion*ess* who does most of the killing). The cheetah, fastest of all land animals, was so effective that it was taken on hunts from the reigns of pharaoh to Medici. All across the world the animal kingdom has a healthy respect for the prowess of the Ocelot, Panther, Leopard, Puma, Jaguar.

Even in the quiet and safe domestic situation the oldest tom can still rouse himself for the inquisitive mouse. The nursing queen will leave her kindle of kittens to bring back samples of her skills.

And while we're all masters of the chase, some of our ranks have risen to exalted heights.

Minnie, of White City Stadium, London, dealt with 12480 mice between 1927 and 1933. **Mickey**, guard of Shepherd & Sons, Ltd., Burscough, Lancashire, disposed of 22000 mice in 23 years. And **Towser**, the much-missed mouser extraordinaire of Glenturret Distillery, Crieff, Perthshire, nailed 25000 mice from 1963 to 1986.

And these are just the recorded, verified bags of recent years. Who knows how many rodents we disposed of for the Egyptians? Who can estimate how many more plague-carrying rats we could've spared Europe if not for that darkest of dark ages wiping out so many of our kind?

Foolishly, some societies have tried to control rodents without us. The Greeks tried weasels and stone martens before realising these creatures killed everything, indiscriminately. And in the 13th Century the Japanese began to think that mere *representations* of cats would deter vermin from their crops and precious silk stores, without the real thing, like some kind of scarecrow. Bad move.

And finally, it could even be said that cats helped discover the New World, since before our addition to ships' crews their wanderings were limited to how far they could sail before the rats finished off their food supplies.

No, history has shown there really is no substitute for the domestic Cat, hunter on a small scale perhaps, but hunter supreme.

Catanatomy

The smallest feline is a masterpiece.
— *Leonardo da Vinci*

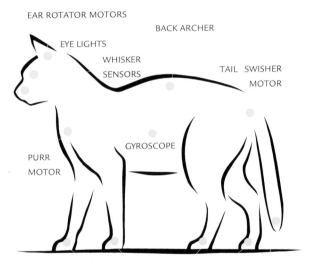

EAR ROTATOR MOTORS

BACK ARCHER

EYE LIGHTS

WHISKER
SENSORS

TAIL SWISHER
MOTOR

GYROSCOPE

PURR
MOTOR

CLAW RETRACTOR MOTORS

TAIL -END
TWITCHER

The Hunt

For those weaned too early to have learned this from their mothers, here are the pertinent steps in becoming a working carnivore, Nature's predator par excellence:

1. Locate prey.

2. Stalk to within striking distance.

3. Freeze and sneer.

4. Crouch on front paws, raise bottom.

5. Swish tail from side to side.

6. Narrow eyes.

7. Stutter and drool.

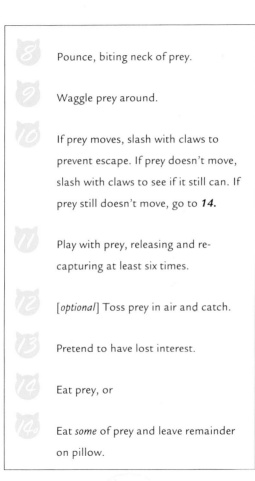

8 Pounce, biting neck of prey.

9 Waggle prey around.

10 If prey moves, slash with claws to prevent escape. If prey doesn't move, slash with claws to see if it still can. If prey still doesn't move, go to **14.**

11 Play with prey, releasing and re-capturing at least six times.

12 [*optional*] Toss prey in air and catch.

13 Pretend to have lost interest.

14 Eat prey, or

14a Eat *some* of prey and leave remainder on pillow.

The Cat in Art

PREHISTORIC

Lascaux Caves, France c.1300BC

EGYPTIAN

Limestone stela, Eighth Dynasty, c.2276BC

GREEK

Amphora by Mykattides c.510-500BC

ROMAN

Capital from the Temple of Felixus Maximus c.300BC

MAYA

Petroglyph c.700

INDIAN

The God Sastht, Punjai c.1000

ye Catte

MEDIÆVAL

Wood engraving attributed to the monk Marmaladus, c.1150

RENAISSANCE

Leopardo da Vinci, pen and ink, c.1510

JAPANESE

Watercolour on silk, Nekomura, c.1790

CUBIST

Pablo Picatso, *La Derrière du Chat*, 1908

18

FUTURIST

Wasily Katdinsky, *Cat in Motion*, 1918

MODERNIST

Jackson Pollock, *Cat No. 5*, 1949

A kitten is so flexible that she is almost double; the hind parts
are equivalent to another kitten with which the forepart plays.
She does not discover that her tail belongs to her
until you tread on it.

— *Henry David Thoreau*

When bored, chew the edges of
important documents.

When tense, chase tail.

When resentful, play noisily at 3am.

When neglected, scratch something.

When perky, climb the curtains.

When randy, spray.

When hungry, stick nose in ear of sleeping host.

When lonely, meow incessantly.

When wanted, hide in remote,
undiscoverable places.

When boisterous, tease the dog,
or harass the hamster.

When offended, pee in houseplant pots,
cupboards or shoes.

When curious, explore dustbins.

When in trouble, purr.

Catalogue of Famous Felines

There are no ordinary cats.

— *Colette*

Cat actors

The most famous feline thespian in the UK is **Arthur**, star of 30 *Spillers Kattomeat* commercials, in which he magnificently scooped cat food out of a tin from 1966 to 1975. He died in 1976 and was succeeded by Arthur II.

His US counterpart is **Morris** from the *9 Lives* cat food commercials, who died in 1978 and was in turn replaced with Morris II.

Cartoon cats

Because of our wonderful personalities, we cats are often immortalised in popular art, most notably cartoons. **Krazy Kat**, by George Herriman, graced Hearst Newspapers beginning in 1910.

Felix, attributed to Pat Sullivan in the 1920's, was the first sound cartoon and became more popular than Charlie Chaplin, Harold Lloyd or Buster Keaton. **Sylvester**, whose first film screened in 1944, was actually awarded an Oscar in 1947. (It was Tweetie-Pie, the canary in his films, who is renowned for saying, 'I taut I taw a puddy tat!') A similar role was **Tom** of the hundreds of Tom and Jerry films. **Fritz the Cat**, a tougher, more street-wise feline, was first drawn by Robert Crumb in *Comix* and filmed by Ralph Bakshi in both 1972 and '74. Currently, of course, there's the famous (or perhaps infamous) **Garfield**, by Jim Davis, who created his insightful character in the US in 1978.

Charmion

We know next to nothing about Cleopatra's cat, but there's irony in Cleo having been a cat lover. A Roman soldier accidentally killed a cat in Egypt (where cats were, of course, revered), was tortured, dragged through the town and hanged. This triggered a war between the two countries, ending in the deaths of Cleopatra and her Roman lover Anthony.

The Cheshire Cat

In Lewis Carroll's *Alice in Wonderland*, the Cheshire Cat gives Alice skewed advice through riddles. It appears grin-first and leaves grin-last, and though fictional serves as a symbol of the cat's intelligence and sly cunning. Also, perhaps, our tendency to patronise. It's thought that Carroll got the idea from the cat's head stamped on a brand of Cheshire cheese popular at the time.

Dick Whittington's cat

In the early 15th Century little Dickie came from Gloucestershire to seek his fortune in London. Some versions of the story say his cat went with him, others that all he could afford from his meagre scullion's wages was a cat to keep his garret rat-free. Anyway, when one day the other servants put up money to invest in their employer's trading ship, Dick contributed his only possession — his cat.

On its arrival at one of the Spice Islands, the cat promptly cleaned up the king's ratbag of a palace, and the grateful ruler gave the cat's 'owner' a fortune in return for the cat's continued services .

Dick went on to thrice become Lord Mayor of London, but not much is ever said about the cat's later life on the island. Actually the clever creature was pregnant when she arrived, and went on to give birth to several striking litters, who spread her line throughout the East, the descendants of which are now imported back into the West at exorbitant prices.

Graymalkin

One of the spirits invoked to serve the witches at the beginning of Shakespeare's *Macbeth*, this cat doesn't appear much, being more of a symbolic, magic prop. Its role per-

petuates the myth of cats being somehow evil, but then what would you expect from Scotland, where peasants up to the end of the Middle Ages were authorised to kill us and use our fur for clothing.

Graymalkin is only referred to once again by

Thrice the brinded [brindled, tabby] cat hath mew'd.

A cat of another kind is mentioned later in

Add thereto a tiger's chaudron [entrails],
For the ingredients of our cauldron.

(A contrived rhyme, Will, if ever we've heard one.)

Malkin had long been a word meaning female cat. *Grimalkin* predated Macbeth as a moniker for an old she-cat or, by extension, a spiteful old woman.

Maneki-Neko

Famous in Japan, Maneki (*Neko* means Cat) is the small female cat who lures and enchants, bringing happiness and good luck. She is nearly always shown with left paw raised in greeting and benediction, and is the model for the phenomenally successful 'Hello Kitty' line of charms and toys. Ceramic Maneki-Nekos are given to new businesses and home-owners to attract good fortune and prosperity.

Puss-in-Boots

In this 1697 story by Charles Perrault, a witty and flamboyant cat manages through its exploits to defeat a giant, make a peasant boy into the Marquis of Carabas, and allows him to marry a princess. Perrault adapted tales dating from Italian, Arabic and Sanskrit sources, showing the persistence of the belief that cats bring luck and good fortune.

Schrödinger's Cat

Erwin Schrödinger, Nobel prize-winning physicist, described a hypothetical paradox linking the fate of a cat to the state of a simple quantum system.

A cat, he proposed, is placed in a box containing a bottle of poison, and the poison is released with a 50/50 probability linked to the outcome of a quantum event such as the decay/non-decay of a radioactive atom, or the up/down spin of an electron.

The laws of physics state that *until an observer looks in the box* the quantum system is in a hybrid of all possible states. Is the cat, therefore, also in a hybrid dead/alive state until observed?

Personally, we think the man should've been reported to the RSPCA. Hypothetical or not, this is an experiment of extreme cruelty, and should never have been suggested in case some literal-minded physics student actually tries it.

Tabitha

In June of 1994 Tabitha and her sister Pandora were travelling in their respective cat carriers (or in Pandora's case, presumably a box) on a flight from New York to Los Angeles.

On arrival, only Pandora was where she was supposed to be. Tabitha had escaped somewhere, and for twelve days became a kind of *claws célèbre* as dozens of humans searched for her.

32,000 miles later she was eventually located, two pounds lighter, by a psychic who had predicted her whereabouts in the cargo area ceiling.

Tom, the original

Prior to 1760 male cats were called 'Ram' cats, and then along came Tom the Cat in *The Life and Adventures of a Cat*. Were it not for this timely publication, we'd still be stuck with being known as either Rams or Dams, blunt and offensive terms referring solely to our reproductive roles. Sometimes one can still hear the term, 'That dam cat,' but this is luckily a rare and archaic holdover from the past.

White Heather

Queen Victoria's cat is thought to have triggered the monarch's famous 'We are not amused,' when caught toying with Prince Albert's toupée.

then there are the famous humans who professed to never be without their faithful felines...

Sesostris, an Ethiopian, is credited as the person who brought cats into Egypt after the conquest of Nubia. The **Egyptians** then worshipped the cat goddess *Bastet* (or *Pasht*, from which it's said we get *puss*), daughter of Isis and Osiris, from 3000BC. Bastet reigned 2000 years, during which it was illegal, upon pain of death, to smuggle cats out of the country. **Cleopatra** modelled her eye makeup on the eyes of a cat.

It's quite possible that the reason Ireland has no snakes is not just the arrival of **St Patrick**, but the fact that he brought with him cats.

In the Middle Ages a short-lived cult grew up around the Norse goddess of love **Freyia**, Freyja or Freya, who had two black cats pulling her chariot. This unfortunately just fueled (literally) more persecution, at a time when any religion other than Christianity was pronounced Pagan and attacked.

Mohammed truly appreciated cats. Legend has it that once, rather than disturb his favourite *Muezza* as she slept in his arms, he cut off his sleeve. Muezza awoke and bowed in thanks, and Mohammed passed his hand three times down her back in blessing, giving all cats henceforth immunity from the dangers of falling.

Although popular with **Buddhists**, the cat is not included in Buddhist writings allegedly because one of our kind happened to fall asleep during Buddha's funeral. Well, we all loved the man, but what did they expect? Those festivities just went on for ever. There's a limit to how many gongs and saffron robes one can take, after all.

Pliny the Elder wrote about cats, as did **Cicero**, the Roman orator of the first century BC. **Leonardo da Vinci** understandably loved us too, and **Isaac Newton** paid us the honour of inventing the cat flap, or cat door (probably at the request of his cat master) and was knighted for his brilliance. Whereas **Julius Cæsar, Alexander the Great, Genghis Khan, Henry III** of France, **Napoleon Bonaparte, Mussolini** and **Adolf Hitler**

are said to have hated us, which goes to show we're only disliked by those who should themselves be despised.

Owen Gould, British consul general in Bangkok, was given two Siamese cats by the King of Siam in 1884, and when shipped back to England they triggered a fashion that continues to this day.

Wordsworth, Tennyson, Coleridge, Byron, Twain, Keats, Swinburne, Sir Winston Churchill, Admiral Nelson, Cardinals Wolsey and **Richelieu, Borges, Wells, Baudelaire, Martin Luther, Arnold, Hardy, James, Sand, Hugo, Poe, Colette, Lear, Zola, Dr Johnson, T S Eliot, Sir Walter Scott** and **The Brontë Sisters** would only work with their cats around, no doubt to help critique their creations and help with the difficult bits. **Hemingway's** home in Key West, Florida, is still full of felines.

And many a US president has shrewdly kept a cat at his side in the White House. **George Washington, Rutherford B. Hayes, Thomas Jefferson, Herbert Hoover** and **Abraham Lincoln** all required a feline presence in the Oval Office. **Calvin Coolidge** had *Tiger* and *Blacky*, **Theodore**

Roosevelt was advised by *Slippers* and *Tom Quartz*, **Gerald Ford** consulted *Shan*, **Jimmy Carter** relied upon his daughter Amy's *Misty Malarky Ying Yang*, **John F. Kennedy** was sadly a touch allergic but nevertheless kept around Caroline's *Tom Kitten* (and possibly a supply of antihistamines), **Bill Clinton** of course sports *Socks*, First Cat.

JEKYLL   **HYDE**

playful   suspicious   vicious
happy   paranoid   nasty
kittenish   distrustful   brutal
fun   wary   cold
docile   belligerent   warlike

⟵⎯⎯ 2 SECONDS ⎯⎯⟶

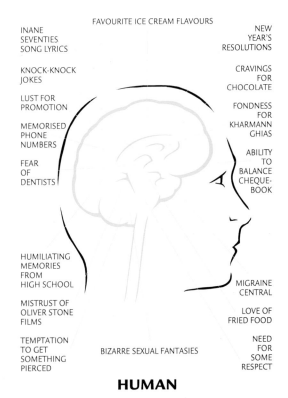

FAVOURITE ICE CREAM FLAVOURS

INANE
SEVENTIES
SONG LYRICS

NEW
YEAR'S
RESOLUTIONS

KNOCK-KNOCK
JOKES

CRAVINGS
FOR
CHOCOLATE

LUST FOR
PROMOTION

FONDNESS
FOR
KHARMANN
GHIAS

MEMORISED
PHONE
NUMBERS

ABILITY
TO
BALANCE
CHEQUE-
BOOK

FEAR
OF
DENTISTS

HUMILIATING
MEMORIES
FROM
HIGH SCHOOL

MIGRAINE
CENTRAL

MISTRUST OF
OLIVER STONE
FILMS

LOVE OF
FRIED FOOD

TEMPTATION
TO GET
SOMETHING
PIERCED

BIZARRE SEXUAL FANTASIES

NEED
FOR
SOME
RESPECT

HUMAN

PLAY

SLEEP

FOOD

SEX

CAT

Cat Aerobics

Kitties — are you living a full feline life?
Work off that widening waistline with this
twenty-step programme.

1 Make sure humans are out.

2 Spray bedroom.

3 Scratch newest piece of furniture.

4 Knock over vase, sniff flowers.

5 Drag flowers around rooms, eat one.

6 Vomit on expensive rug.

7 Drink from tap, unroll all paper towels.

8 Scatter papers on desk.

9 Nap.

10 Sneak out and catch bird or mouse.

>

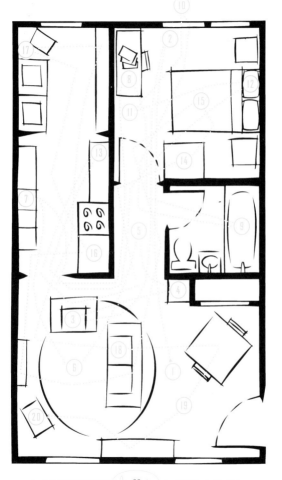

11. Maim and play with animal.

12. Leave dead animal in prominent position.

13. Nap.

14. Climb into wardrobe and shed hair on dress clothing.

15. Relieve self on duvet.

16. Nap.

17. Hide and ignore humans upon return, until fed.

18. Climb onto lap(s), submit to stroking.

19. Swat indifferently at little jingly mouse toy.

20. Curl up on TV, obscuring screen with tail.

Cat Sports

When I play with my cat, who knows whether she isn't
amusing herself with me more than I am with her?
— *Michel Montaigne, Essais*

*Due to our intrinsic dignity, we cats are notoriously hard
for humans to teach tricks. Unless we're in the mood,
that is, which is as rare as a smart dog.
But some tricks are our own, and properly performed can
tone muscle, enhance reaction time, and provide a
welcome relief from the boredom of daily routine.
Here are some of the most popular, rated by difficulty:*

Fencewalking *(2.0. Easy)*

Walking along fences comes relatively easily to
us, enabling us to escape pursuit and serving to

show off our sense of balance to the Bigs and other lower orders.

Passing another on a fence *(9.7. Tricky)* is a variation for experts, requiring either *a*) acrobatics, *b*) aggression, or *c*) sex.

Treeleaping *(4.8. Moderate.)*

Leaping up trees is a survival tactic turned sport, simple for our power springs to accomplish and providing a position eminently suitable to our superiority.

Getting back down *(8.9. Nasty)* can be a problem, however, since unlike squirrels we prefer not to descend head-first. It is thus sometimes necessary to enlist the rest of your household into participating with outstretched arms or a ladder.

The Linoleum Slide *(5.3. Potentially risky.)*

Sliding along floors is often at first inadver-

tent, following a fresh waxing by your staff. Swift and exhilarating, not all slides can be controlled and as a consequence can end in sudden surprise impacts with kitchen appliances. Practise, though, can provide slalom skills and a measure of steering.

Tableskidding *(5.3. Requires practise.)*

This event is related to the Linoleum Slide, being comprised of essentially the same moves, but involves an added leap to a table to see what's on top. If what's on top is a tablecloth, a satisfying

glissade can be obtained, sometimes at the cost of some servants' ugly crockery. No real loss.

The Curtain Climb (7.8. *Exhausting but fun.*)

Clambering up cloth is a natural for confined cats, providing a good outlet for energies in a short, controlled burst of spectacular action. Luckily your housekeepers will have provided hanging sheets of the stuff for your exercise.

Naturally those who have been declawed, or even recently trimmed, should not attempt this or any other climbing events.

Dogteasing (8.5. *Moderately risky, depending on personality of canine.*)

Teasing dogs, so natural that we suspect it's genetically programmed within us, can take as many forms as your imagination can muster. Eating a dog's food, swiping at a sleeping dog's nose, even the simple showing of one's rear to a canine can infuriate it to apoplexy and trigger a good chase.

Of course, before beginning you must be sure you're faster, or you should limit your teasing to dogs outside your (closed) window. And never assume that all big dogs are slow, nor all small dogs a pushover.

The Keyboard Bounce (9.1. *Requires speed and accuracy.*)

The Big bipeds who clean your home like to sit in front of picture boxes. One they just watch (often while eating), the other they tap keys in front of.

This second type is the desired target. Simply leap onto the keys and off again, but make sure you turn in time to catch the expression on the human's face. For some obscure reason this trick upsets them to a hilarious degree.

The Bounce can also be applied to musical
instruments with more or less the same effect.

The Birdcage Swing

(9.5. Requires accuracy.)

If you share your
residence with a bird
it's probably already
twitchy when you're
around. So why not
traumatise it perma-
nently and exercise at
the same time? Just
leap at its cage and
swing for a while until

you get bored, then drop nonchalantly to the floor. (As long as it's a suspended cage, that is. Forget the ones on pedestals.)

In the absence of a caged bird, a hanging plant will suffice, though it won't react as well. Don't be tempted to substitute a ceiling fan, chandelier or party ornaments.

The Street Streak *(9.9. Potentially suicidal.)*

Outdoor cats inevitably have to cross streets full of Bigs driving boxes on wheels, and this is no mean feat. A danger even to themselves, they constitute a serious hazard to the feline race.

Do not try to outdodge these vehicles unless you have youth, agility and distance on your side, and *never* try to dodge more than one at a time. Watch out for the two-wheeled versions too, and for those surprise potholes in the road.

If in doubt, better to take the long way home, or forego the exercise entirely. Better a fat cat than a *flat* cat.

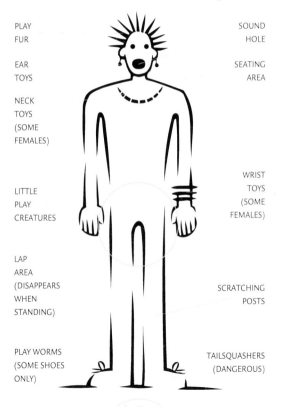

PLAY
FUR

EAR
TOYS

NECK
TOYS
(SOME
FEMALES)

LITTLE
PLAY
CREATURES

LAP
AREA
(DISAPPEARS
WHEN
STANDING)

PLAY WORMS
(SOME SHOES
ONLY)

SOUND
HOLE

SEATING
AREA

WRIST
TOYS
(SOME
FEMALES)

SCRATCHING
POSTS

TAILSQUASHERS
(DANGEROUS)

The Ten Steps to Good Grooming

Don't forget —
it's important to follow this sequence exactly.

Lick lips.

Lick paw.

Rub wet paw over side of head.

Lick other paw.

Rub wet paw over other side of head.

Lick front legs and shoulders.

Lick flanks.

Lick private parts.

Lick hind legs.

Lick tail.

optional extra:

Lick humans.

Ask Smudge

SMUDGE

Now to answer a few questions from your staff...

Dear Smudge —

My cat refuses to sleep in the nice basket I bought her, and will only sleep in my sock drawer. If I try to keep it closed she yowls until I open it again. What can I do?

— Bedless in Birmingham

Dear Bedless —

Obviously 'your' cat has decided the sock drawer *is* her bed. Sounds fine to me. Get used to it. Use the basket for fruit or dried flowers.

Dear Smudge —

Our cat always seems to want to play, noisily, in the middle of the night when my husband and I are trying to sleep. What can I do to stop him?

— Sleepless in Scunthorpe

Dear Sleepless —

Why are you and your husband trying to sleep at such an unnatural hour? Obviously 'your' cat has his priorities straight regarding appropriate use of those delicious hours of darkness. Only humans persist in activities during the glare of the day. Switch to the night shift.

Dear Smudge —

My cat suddenly won't eat anything I put in front of her. I'm worried that she's not getting enough nutrition. What should I do?

— Mealless, Melton Mowbray

Dear Mealless —

Been buying that cheapo cat food again? Or washing the bowl with some stinky new detergent? Without more information the possible explanations of why 'your' cat is refusing to eat are too numerous to list. If you've changed catfood lately, change back. Rinse the bowl thoroughly with clean water. And if you're still worried about starvation let the cat out. She'll just dine elsewhere.

Dear Smudge —

My cats have always scratched my sofa and arm-chairs. Eventually I had to buy new furniture, and now they've started on these too. I tried a scratching post but they're not interested. What can I do?

— Shredded, Stoke Poges

Dear Shredded —

What's the problem? Sofas *are* for scratching, aren't they? The cushions are for sitting, and the sides are for scratching, right? You could try wrapping some of the same material around a log of wood, or sit on bean bags instead. But no guarantees. Claws need keeping in shape, after all.

Dear Smudge —

There's hair everywhere. Everywhere! My boyfriend is sneezing, my best clothes are covered, and my flat looks like a kind of fur farm. Should I do as my boyfriend says and get rid of my cat?

— Hairy in Harlow

Dear Hairy —

If you want a bald pet, get a frog. But you wanted soft sensuality, silky elegance and fluffy cuddliness so you got a cat. Get a new boyfriend. He'll lose his hair too, eventually, and *his* won't grow back.

Dear Smudge —

My cat has an aggression problem. He terrorises the other cats in the area, gets into scrapes with most of the dogs, and now the neighbours are starting to complain. What's the solution?

— War Zone, Wapping

Dear War Zone —

You have the honour of housing a feline Wellington or Patton, and certainly there are drawbacks to sharing a home with such a dynamic personality. But such is the Great Pecking Order of Life, and you happen to have a *Pecker* (if you'll pardon the expression), rather than a *Peckee*. I suggest judicious and generous payoffs to the injured.

Dear Smudge —

My business is based in my home, and every time I try to work my cat interferes with everything I do. He plays with my pen, sits in front of the computer screen and knocks the phone off its hook. Does my cat have a personality disorder?

— Exasperated in Exmouth

Dear Exasperated —

'Your' cat obviously craves more affection than you've been giving him. Stop crunching numbers or whatever stupid, inane work you waste your time on and pay some attention to the feline of the house. The only personality disorder is in blind subservience to making a living at the cost of domestic, or in your case business, bliss. Take a break and stroke the cat.

Dear Smudge —

Sometimes our cat returns from her neighbourhood travels and brings her chums back through the cat door. They then proceed to party in our kitchen till all hours spraying, howling, making love and eating everything that's not nailed down. What do we do? Stop letting the cat out? Close up the cat flap?

— Partied Out, Pontypridd

Dear Partied Out —

Sounds great to me. I have your address. See you next Saturday.

Dear Smudge —

Even though I've made it clear I'm not impressed, my cat keeps bringing home small, recently killed animals. How can I stop him doing this?

— Slaughterhouse in Surbiton

Dear Slaughterhouse —

Remember that cats are predators and carnivores. When we see a mouse, for instance...*eyes glowing like amber coals behind slitted lids, the wiry muscles of Shere Khan the tiger flex beneath his flank as he leaps from the elephant grass and sinks his hunt-honed fangs into...oh, sorry. Got a bit carried away there. Well, you get the picture.*

Dear Smudge —

I live alone without companionship, and though I'd like company I'm reluctant to commit to the responsibility of a pet. Are cats a lot of fuss and bother?

— **Lonely, Loughborough**

Dear Lonely —

Want a low maintenance pet? Get a glove puppet. Or a smurf. For a live, loving companion, get yourself a cat. Decorative, self-cleaning, self-exercising, affectionate and with a relatively small appetite, nothing will ever beat the feline for friendship.

also available in the same series:

HUMANS AS PETS

MYSTERY OF CATS

by David Westwood,
author of THE OFFICE MANUAL and THE LOVE MANUAL

TWO HEADS PUBLISHING

9 Whitehall Park

London N19 3TS

ISBN 1 897850 71 9

Printed in Great Britain by Caldra House Ltd., Hove, Sussex